WBB DEC 6 - 1999

J 796.912092 Smi

Smith, Pohla.

Superstars of men's
figure skating /

DISCARDED

PALM BEACH COUNTY
LIBRARY SYSTEM
3650 SUMMIT BLVD.
WEST PALM BEACH, FLORIDA 33406

AF479333

MALE SPORTS STARS

Superstars of Men's Figure Skating

Superstars of Men's Pro Wrestling

Superstars of Men's Soccer

Superstars of Men's Swimming and Diving

Superstars of Men's Tennis

Superstars of Men's Track and Field

CHELSEA HOUSE PUBLISHERS

SUPERSTARS OF MEN'S FIGURE SKATING

Pohla Smith

CHELSEA HOUSE PUBLISHERS
Philadelphia

Produced by Daniel Bial and Associates
New York, New York

Picture research by Alan Gottlieb
Cover illustration by Bill Vann

frontispiece photo: Scott Hamilton

Copyright 1998 by Chelsea House Publishers, a division of Main Line Book Co.
All rights reserved. Printed and bound in the United States of America.

First Printing

1 3 5 7 9 8 6 4 2

Library of Congress Cataloging-in-Publication Data

Smith, Pohla.
    Superstars of men's figure skating / Pohla Smith.
      p.   cm. — (Male sports stars)
    Includes bibliographical references (p.) and index.
    Summary: Provides a look at the skating careers of such performers
as Dick Button, John Curry, Scott Hamilton, and Brian Boitano.
    ISBN 0-7910-4586-2 (hc)
    1. Skaters—Biography—Juvenile literature. [1. Ice skaters.]
I. Title. II. Series.
GV850.A2S545   1998
796.91'2'0810922—dc21
[B]   97-42878
                                       CIP
                                       AC

CONTENTS

CHAPTER 1
DICK BUTTON   7

CHAPTER 2
THE JENKINS BROTHERS   13

CHAPTER 3
JOHN CURRY   23

CHAPTER 4
SCOTT HAMILTON   31

CHAPTER 5
THE BATTLE OF THE BRIANS   43

CHAPTER 6
THE NEW GENERATION   53

CHRONOLOGY   62
FURTHER READING   63
INDEX   64

1

DICK BUTTON

Richard Totten Button didn't look much like a future two-time Olympic figure skating champion as a kid. At age 12, the boy from Englewood, New Jersey, looked more like the kid no one wants on his basketball team in gym class. He stood 5' 2" and weighed 162 pounds—in other words, short and overweight. He also was a bit clumsy.

Dick had been skating since he was about five years old, using his brothers' hand-me-down skates to bump over a frozen pond. When it turned out that Dick was quite good, he worked hard at it, spending hours practicing jumps and mastering the school figures that were then mandatory for competitive skaters.

When Button was 12 years old, he started taking lessons from skating coach Gus Lussi. Gus,

Dick Button performing at the 1948 world championships in Davos, Switzerland. That year he won the American, European, Olympic, and world championships.

who later coached Dorothy Hamill, would be the only coach Dick ever had. Gus was the only coach Dick ever needed.

Lussi was a former ski jumper from Switzerland with great knowledge of the science of physics and its effect on jumps and spins. Dick was the perfect athlete to try the moves Gus dreamed up, for he had courage, great enthusiasm, and strong ankles. They were a perfect team to dominate and reshape figure skating into a much more athletic and daring sport.

In time, Dick lost all his excess weight and his tendency toward awkwardness. He grew to be 6 feet tall and a trim 172 pounds, and developed into a graceful yet explosive free skater. He was capable of jumping higher than any of his competitors.

At age 16, Dick became the youngest man in history to win the United States figure skating championship. And two years after that, in 1948, when Dick was an 18-year-old freshman at Harvard University, he became the first American to win the Olympic figure skating championship.

At those Winter Games, he also became the first man to perform a double axel jump, a move in which the skater spins 2 1/2 times in the air. Today, the top male skaters do triple axels, but back then it was the most spectacular move the skating world had ever seen.

Amazingly, Dick had never completed the jump successfully until two days before the Olympic finals. A more cautious man might have practiced much longer before using the jump in competition. If he had fallen, he would have blown his chances of winning the gold medal. Dick, however, was anything but cautious.

Later, he said in a book about his career and

Button introduced many jumps to the repertoire. Here he is seen practicing in Colorado Springs, Colorado.

skating that he wished he had been better pre-pared with the double axel. But he said he was sickened by the thought "of backing away from something because of the pressure of the Olympic games . . . Once I had made up my mind, I could not divert the steps that culminated in the dou-ble axel."

The jump went fine.

Over the next four years of his amateur career, fans got accustomed to seeing Dick invent new moves that eventually became standard for all competitive skaters. One was the flying camel, a jump spin in which the skater holds his legs split at right angles to one another. He also did the first triple jump in history (a triple loop); the first back-to-back double axels; and the first back-to-back-to-back double loop jumps, a three-jump combination that is still rarely seen.

Fans across the world also got accustomed to

seeing Dick win every competition he entered. In 1948, he became the only man to hold the Olympic, world, European, United States, and North American championships at one time.

With typical bravado, Dick introduced his back-to-back double axels while successfully competing for the 1950 world championship in Wembley, England. He completed his first triple loop while going for his second Olympic championship at the 1952 Winter Games in Oslo, Sweden.

Button freely admitted in his book *Dick Button on Skates* that he had been extremely nervous about trying the historic triple.

"I forgot in a momentary panic which shoulder should go forward and which back," he said. "I was extraordinarily conscious of the judges, who looked so immobile at rinkside. But this was it. . . . The wind cut my eyes, and the coldness caused tears to stream down my cheeks. Up! Up! Height was vital. Round and round again in a spin which took only a fraction of a second to complete before it landed on a clean, steady, back edge. I pulled away breathless, excited, and overjoyed, as applause rolled from the faraway stands like the rumbling of a distant pounding sea."

After the 1952 season, Dick turned professional and skated with the Ice Capades and Holiday on Ice shows. By that time he had won a total of seven American, three North American, one European, five world, and two Olympic titles.

Fans and experts alike had expected to see Dick turn pro two years before he did, after he won the 1950 world title. But, unlike most amateurs today who train full-time for the Olympics, Dick had squeezed in his training between studies at Harvard University. They were equally important to him.

"Think I'm crazy enough to sweat through two years of Harvard and then not finish?" he answered when asked about turning pro after the 1950 season.

Later, Dick earned his law degree from Harvard, too. It proved of great use after his pro skating days were over. He became a producer-promoter of sports shows, especially professional ice competitions. He still produces such shows today.

Dick also has had a long and successful secondary career as a television commentator. His explanations and commentary—along with those of his long-time announcing partner, Peggy Fleming—have taught millions of fans about the fine points of figure skating and today's top skaters.

★

2

THE JENKINS BROTHERS

Even after Dick Button retired as a competitive skater, U.S. men stayed on top of the figure skating world for a long time. The next skaters to keep winning the major trophies were two brothers from Akron, Ohio: Hayes Alan Jenkins and David Jenkins.

Hayes's and David's father was a lawyer for Goodyear, the tire manufacturer and largest employer in Akron. He had been a good athlete as a youth. Their mother was very gifted musically. Hayes and David inherited both talents.

The primary reason the Jenkins brothers started skating when they were children was that all of their friends went skating every Saturday morning. They skated at a big rink owned and operated by the Akron Skating Club.

Hayes started taking lessons after his older sister, Nancy, started lessons. The family jokes

After Dick Button retired from amateur competition, Hayes Alan Jenkins (right) and his brother David continued America's domination in the sport.

that David then had no choice but to take lessons as well—he was too young to stay home by himself while their parents were at the rink with Hayes and Nancy.

Nancy preferred pairs and ice dancing to singles, and Hayes was drafted as her partner. They competed as high as junior nationals, the division right below the seniors who go to the Olympics. They were eighth at their first junior pair nationals in 1945, and for the next three years, they continued to compete nationally in all of the major figure skating categories: singles, pairs, and dance.

"It made competitions pretty hectic," Hayes said. But, though it took a lot of time and energy, the schedule left Hayes little time for worrying about competitions. "Sometimes it's better to be busy," he said.

By that time, the Jenkins siblings were traveling to nearby Cleveland to get more advanced coaching during the school year. During the summers, they went to Lake Placid, New York to take lessons from Dick Button's coach, Gus Lussi.

Hayes's careers in ice dancing and pairs skating ended when Nancy went to college and retired from competition. He then concentrated on singles and soon was a rising young star. He won his first gold medal, the U.S. Junior Men's title, in 1948, soon after his 15th birthday. That earned him a spot on the 1949 U.S. world team, and he made his first trip to Europe to compete when he was only a sophomore in high school. It was a trip he would make seven more times.

For the first four years, though, Hayes was the number-three guy on the American team, an apprentice to champion Dick Button and number-two American Jimmy Grogan. Over that time,

Hayes won three U. S. men's bronze medals and one silver. He was also the North American bronze medalist in 1949 and 1951 and world bronze medalist in 1950 and 1952. He placed fourth at the 1956 Olympics. The winner of all of those competitions was Dick Button.

"I wanted to win, and, certainly to win I'd have to beat Dick," Hayes remembered of his long apprenticeship. "And I can't say I ever presumed I could beat Dick. I did feel I could give him a run for his money."

Hayes was lucky in that he never had any major illness or injury to overcome. The toughest problem he faced was finances. Back then, the United States Figure Skating Association didn't provide financial aid to anyone but the national champion. Hayes's family had to pay for everything—not just his lessons and ice time, but also all of the expenses involved with traveling to Europe to compete.

The family's expenses continued to mount after Hayes won his first title in 1953, because at that time David started climbing in the ranks. Three years younger than Hayes, David qualified for the 1954 world team by winning the junior national title. Hayes and David would skate together on three U.S. world teams and the 1956 Olympic team.

"It certainly was very expensive," David said. "My family sacrificed financial security when we virtually ran out of money."

But, Hayes noted, "My parents never burdened my brother and me with that part of it."

By the time the money was running out, the famous Broadmoor Skating Club in Colorado Springs, Colorado, came to the rescue and offered to sponsor the Jenkins brothers. Though that is

*Hayes Jenkins performs a
flying camel.*

a common occurrence now, it was somewhat controversial 45 years ago. The brothers and their mother moved to Colorado Springs. David enrolled in the local high school, where skaters were required to make the honor roll if they wanted to get out early each day for practice.

Hayes, who had two quarters of study at Northwestern University behind him, transferred to Colorado College. David later followed him there. Both had academic scholarships.

The brothers said they never felt any rivalry toward each other. Rather, their relationship was one of love for and pride in each other.

"It was never spoken, though," Hayes said. "Other than in the '56 Olympics, when it was all over and we were waiting for the marks. There were no computers then and it took a while. David turned to me and said, 'If you don't win I'm never going to skate again.'"

David also remembers that moment. "It embarrassed him. He was trying to shut me up. It was tough to watch him skate. It was like a parent watching children. I don't think my stomach was relaxed for several weeks after I watched my brother," he said.

"I think one reason Hayes and I never had any competition between us was that we were so different," David added. "Some people liked my skating; some liked his. I would never have dreamed of beating him then." As David explained earlier, his artistry took longer to develop than his athleticism.

Hayes was also forced into playing the role of big brother/father when the two were traveling to competitions. But, again, there seems to have been no resentment. "For the first couple years, I was too busy trying to look after him, making sure he didn't lose his passport and things like that," Hayes said.

"Yeah, and he'd see if my skates were polished and my blades were sharpened," David said. "I always knew if I didn't do it, he would."

David said Hayes also was his role model—something much tougher for David to deal with. "He was hard to live up to because we weren't constituted the same way. I deeply admired him, but I found him a tough image to live up to."

An example of that came when David was in junior high. His brother was already very serious about his skating, but David wasn't quite sure it was the right thing for him.

"Hayes was a self-starter. I fought it more," David said. "I think it was when I was in the seventh, eighth grades and older, I recognized it was hard to fit in with my peers and have a normal life spending so much time skating."

In 1953, Dick Button retired and Hayes succeeded him as U.S. and world champion. He went on to defend each title three more years and capped his career by winning the 1956 Olympic gold medal at the Winter Games in Cortina, Italy. Then he went to law school, skating for a couple of summers between terms as a professional and turning the spotlight over to his little brother.

David won four U.S. and three world titles and the 1960 Olympic title before he retired to finish medical school. He skated professionally one year during a leave of absence between his second and third years of medical school to earn money for tuition.

They became the first and only brothers to win successive Olympic championships. Because of Button and the Jenkins brothers, the United States held the world title for 12 straight years, from 1948 through 1959. David Jenkins probably would have won the title in 1960, too, but after winning the Olympics, he was afraid to take any more time off from classes and skipped the competition.

No nation has dominated men's figure skating for that long since.

But Hayes and David are remembered for much more than the large number of titles and medals they won. Like Button, each put his own mark on the shape and style of figure skating.

Hayes could do the same jumps as Dick Button, but he also worked hard on style and was very good at interpreting the music.

"I was maybe a little more of a stylist," Hayes said in an interview in 1997. "I was part of the evolution. Dick introduced athleticism. I think I enjoyed skating to music. Music was very important to me when I skated. I think my contribution was to try to marry athleticism with the classical lines. . . .

"Dick genuinely revolutionized the sport," Hayes added. "No other contribution then could be quite so dramatic. And then skating began to build on that foundation. I think I was part of that."

On the other hand, David, who was shorter and wiry, was more of a daredevil than a stylist. He eventually was able to do every jump possible as a triple, though he was not consistent enough to use his triple axel in competition. In that way, he helped figure skating continue to evolve as an athletic activity.

"I loved to jump," David said in an interview, also in 1997. "I skated like a hockey player. I loved to fall. I loved to jump. Style and that sort of thing was more of a discipline that came to me later."

It had been easier for Hayes to achieve both his sports and academic goals. He finished college in 1956, the same year he won the Olympics. Then he retired and went on to Harvard Law School. David, meanwhile, was a sophomore at Colorado College when he joined his brother on the medals podium to receive the 1956 Olympic bronze medal.

"I had no intention of staying in skating when I went to medical school, and I didn't train for 1959. Then six weeks before the [nationals] competition, I started to skate and I snuck off and missed about three days of school to attend nationals and worlds," David said. "I thought school officials didn't know what I was doing."

They did, of course, but David kept up with his classmates at Western Reserve University in Cleveland, Ohio, so no harm was done. When school let out for the summer of 1959, he started training in earnest for the Olympics, which were to be held in Squaw Valley, California.

Unfortunately, another skater accidentally cut him with a blade, severing a nerve in David's right leg. He was put in a cast and kept off the ice until Christmas. Looking back now, it seems that that should not have been enough time to train for Olympic competition just two months later. But David didn't see it that way.

"It took some of the pressure off me," he said. "The second year of medical school is the hardest." The injury allowed him to get through the first semester before he began serious training with Hayes, who drove from Akron to help David train in Cleveland.

Somehow it all came together. As usual, David trailed after compulsory figures. But his free skating was more than enough to get him the gold. "I'm so happy I could cry," he told reporters back then. "I think it was the best I've ever skated."

After a year skating with the Ice Follies, David returned to Western Reserve and got his medical degree. He became a gastroenterologist, a doctor who specializes in problems with the digestive system. He doesn't skate very often, but he did serve as team doctor for the 1984 U.S. Olympic figure skating team.

In 1956, Hayes Jenkins (right) won the Olympic and world championships while David finished third in both competitions.

Since retiring from medicine in 1996, he has been learning to play golf, bicycling with his wife in Europe, and taking a variety of college classes just for the fun of it.

After graduating from Harvard Law School, Hayes practiced law in a private firm for a few years. Then he followed his father to Goodyear Rubber, where he stayed until his retirement in 1997. He doesn't skate much either, but he does keep up with the sport. His wife is 1960 Olympic champion Carol Heiss, now a very successful skating coach in Cleveland.

3

JOHN CURRY

Sometimes when parents say "no" to a kid's request, it just makes the kid want that thing more.

As a child, what John Curry really wanted to do was dance. He asked his parents if he could take ballet lessons. His father said no, even though he was himself a great fan of musical theater. Mr. Curry thought ballet was too "sissy" for a boy.

Then John saw an ice show on television and liked the skating, too. His mother bought him skates for his seventh birthday, and soon he began taking 15-minute lessons once a week at a rink near his home in a suburb of Birmingham, England. He was never allowed to stay after class and skate around with the other kids. John later said that was a good thing. It kept him from picking up any bad habits.

Still, John never forgot about ballet. Even as

John Curry was interested in adding more ballet to figure skating.

a child, he approached skating as a dancer rather than an athlete. A picture of John skating when he was a child shows he had the posture and style of a dancer right from the start.

John's father died when John was 16. Money was short, so he left school. Then he moved to London and took a job in a supermarket. That allowed him to get better coaching than he had had in Birmingham. He also was finally able to take dance classes.

From that time on, John did his best to put ballet and other kinds of dance together with ice skating. John styled himself after a more recent skater from the international style of skating. His hero was Gillis Grafstrom of Sweden, the Olympic champion in 1920 and 1924.

But there was one big difference between Grafstrom and John. Because the sport had grown so much more athletic over the last century, John had to learn to do all the triple jumps and daring spins, too. He didn't particularly like doing them—especially if they didn't fit the music. In fact, he once performed a very controversial exhibition number that had no jumps.

But John knew if he were going to be a champion, he had to master the jumps, too. Then, after he got to the top of the skating world, he thought he could persuade skating to accept more artistry.

It took him a long time to get there. Some coaches and judges made fun of his style as being "effeminate," a fancy word for "sissy." Others loved the smooth, effortless way he floated across the ice but were afraid to admit it publicly.

John talked about the two-faced judges in an interview with *SportsWorld Magazine* the year after he finished low in the standings of the 1974 European and world championships.

"The bias in judging really is a pain," he said. "Of the nine judges in last year's European championships five came up to me afterwards to say that, without doubt, I was the best. They had all put me fourth, but now they were saying I was the best. What do you say to that? Or to someone who says, 'Oh, you deserved to win tonight' but then you look up what they gave you and find it was a 5.7? It makes you want to spit."

He went from coach to coach, hoping to make his jumps so good he could not be denied a championship. Sometimes, he got very frustrated. He did not always get along with the coaches or like the way they would make him tear apart a skill to learn it over. At one point, he even considered leaving skating to accept a scholarship with the Alvin Ailey Dance Company.

After thinking it over, though, John decided he never could be as good a dancer as he was a skater and stuck with his life's work.

Still, there were good things that happened to him during his long struggle. One came in 1973, when Ed Mosler, a wealthy American who had sponsored the training of many American skaters, offered to sponsor Curry too.

Mosler's help enabled Curry to move to the United States and get coaching from Gus Lussi, Dick Button's old coach, as well as from Carlo Fassi, who coached Olympic champions Peggy Fleming and Dorothy Hamill.

At the beginning of the 1976 competitive season, John also enrolled in a class that seemed to change his life dramatically. It was called Erhart Seminar Training, or EST. It was a course designed to make you think positively rather than negatively about yourself, and it was the newest rage in America.

In later years, EST had its detractors. It didn't work for everyone, but it worked for John, making him a tougher competitor mentally. He was unbeatable that season.

He had a fall while winning his fifth straight British championship in 1976, but from there on he was virtually perfect. He put his jumps and spins together with his beautiful skating in a way that judges could not ignore and swept the European, Olympic, and world championships.

Back home in England, he was a national hero. He was the first person to win a Winter Olympic medal of any kind for Great Britain in 12 years. He also was the first Britisher to win an Olympic winter gold and the first to win the men's world figure skating title in 39 years.

Queen Elizabeth named him to the Order of the British Empire, a high honor in Britain that allowed him to use the letters "O.B.E." behind his name.

More important, coaches and skaters began to copy his style. Among those heavily influenced by him was a young boy named Paul Wylie, who grew up to be the 1992 Olympic bronze medalist. As a young skater Wylie had a chance to take two weeks of lessons from Curry while Curry was training at the Broadmoor in Colorado Springs, Colorado for the 1976 Olympics.

"I kid you not, I was a different skater after those two weeks," Wylie said in an interview with Christine Brennan. "I learned what style is. It's not like going around and flicking your hands and kind of smiling at the judges. It's about class

and a deeper sense of perfection."

After his retirement from amateur skating, John received many offers from professional ice companies. But he wasn't interested in skating with the Ice Capades or Ice Follies. He was determined to change professional skating, just as he had changed amateur skating.

At the time, all ice shows were pretty much the same: lots of feathers, sequins, and pretty men and women scooting around the ice like a circus or vaudeville act. John wanted to see ice shows become more like dance recitals or ballet on ice.

The only offers he accepted were a television special and an appearance at a fund-raiser for the U.S. Olympic Committee. He took the latter because his old friend Ed Mosler arranged for him to work on the routine with the great modern dance choreographer Twyla Tharp.

Meanwhile, John was trying to raise enough

After turning professional, Curry skated in many extravaganzas. Here he previews a routine with JoJo Starbuck.

money to stage the ice dancing show of his dreams. By Christmas 1976, he had put together his own ice dance company, John Curry Theatre on Ice, which showed for three months in London. Out of that grew Theatre of Skating II, but that show was cut short when John was hurt in a mugging.

In 1978, he was ready to try the bright lights and tough critics of Broadway in New York. His new show was called "Ice Dancing." It was much too simple a name for a production that was so lavish, dramatic, and daring.

John recruited 12 skaters, including the popular American JoJo Starbuck, to be in his ice-dancing troupe, and then he asked some of the world's top dance choreographers to design dances for them. They created tangos and ballet and modern dance. John hired people to provide appropriate costumes and lighting.

The show opened in December to such enthusiastic audiences that it had to be moved to a larger theatre. Dance critics praised its originality, and national magazines wrote about Curry and his new art form.

But when the show's run ended, Curry didn't have anything to replace it and people lost interest. He told *Dance Magazine*, "I had the ball and I couldn't run with it, so I decided to do some other things. I like to be a realist. I know we all have dreams, and we've got to work like mad to make them come true. But we've also got to be practical."

John turned for a while to acting, appearing in London, on Broadway, and off-Broadway. Skating was still his life, though, and he also did several TV specials in America. Then, in 1984, he brought his ice dancing troupe back, and it performed to enthusiastic crowds in Washington, D.C.; Boston; and New York through 1985. He also found it a permanent home in Vail, Colorado.

Then bad luck struck. First John found himself in terrible financial problems because of what he called "greedy" producers. He lost more than a half-million dollars when he was sued for nonpayment of show-related bills.

Then, late in 1987, John had a blood test and discovered he was HIV-positive. That meant his blood was contaminated with the virus that causes AIDS.

He skated publicly for the last time in November 1989 in a benefit for AIDS research.

He was diagnosed with AIDS in July 1991 and went home to England because he couldn't afford American health care. His aging mother and brother took care of him. He became a sort of hermit.

Later, though, before he died, John went public to talk about AIDS and the need for people to take precautions to avoid getting or passing on the virus.

He was just 44 when he died in April 1994.

4

SCOTT HAMILTON

A playpen couldn't contain Scott Hamilton when he was a toddler. In fact, he was so active and athletic that his dad, Ernie, had to make a lid for his crib. Otherwise, he would get out of it and get into mischief such as climbing onto the refrigerator to sit in a kitchen cabinet.

Once, his father was working on the roof and briefly left the ladder unattended. When he returned, two-year-old Scott was walking along the edge of the roof. Ernie recalls that Scott never cared too much for walking, either. He was too busy running around their house and yard in Bowling Green, Ohio.

Despite Scott's obvious athletic ability, becoming a world-class athlete proved amazingly hard. The major difficulty was a mystifying illness that stunted his growth and almost killed him as a child.

Dorothy and Ernie Hamilton adopted Scott in

In 1976, Scott Hamilton won his first major title, the U.S. Junior Championship.

1958. At that time, the two professors at Bowling Green University already had a 5 1/2-year-old biological daughter named Susan waiting for him at home. She was very happy to have a little brother. Then, later, the Hamiltons adopted one more baby, Steve, who is four years younger than Scott. An assortment of dogs and cats filled out the family.

Scott was a tiny, skinny tot. But he was so busy climbing and running and playing that it didn't seem to matter. Later, though, when he was about five years old, his family realized he had stopped growing.

With that discovery, Scott began four years of scary misery. There were countless visits to doctors and stays in the hospital. He had to wear a feeding tube in his nose that went all the way to his stomach. He had lots of bad-tasting medicines to take. At one point, doctors thought he might be allergic to wheat and ordered him not to eat bread, cookies, or cake. Scott gave up all foods with wheat, but he didn't get any better.

For a long time, nobody seemed to be able to come up with the right reason for Scott's illness. Nor did they seem able to cure it.

Scott got thinner and thinner and weaker and weaker. He was pale and had dark circles under his eyes. Some doctors said he had a life-threatening illness called cystic fibrosis. At one point, Scott was so weak and sickly that the doctors and Scott's parents thought he would die. Scott was old enough to pick up on the air of sadness that surrounded him.

Finally, a neighbor, Dr. Andrew Klepner, got Scott back on the road to health. Dr. Klepner disagreed with the diagnoses Scott received and thought some of the treatments were making Scott worse. He persuaded Scott's parents to take their child to Children's Hospital of Boston in December 1967 for one more set of tests.

There, Dr. Harry Shwachmann decided that Scott didn't have cystic fibrosis. Nor did he have any sort of major intestinal disorder, and Dr. Shwachmann felt that all the restrictive diets his doctors had put him on were making him worse.

Scott went home to Bowling Green with permission to eat anything he wanted. Soon his appetite got much bigger.

The timing couldn't have been better.

Earlier in 1967, Bowling Green University opened an ice skating rink. Dr. Klepner's family joined the skating club, and in November, his daughters took Scott and Susan along. Scott apparently liked it, because when he got back from Boston, he enrolled in classes at the rink in early 1968. He was nine years old.

As he grew older and stronger, he skated more. Soon he was taking lessons every day. Skating helped him gain strength, and though he would never be big—as an adult he's 5' 3" and weighs 115 pounds—he started to grow. He got strong enough that he even started playing ice hockey. Eventually, though, his parents persuaded him to concentrate on figure skating, where his size wasn't such a disadvantage.

Scott quickly began building a collection of medals. In early 1969, he won a Sub-Juvenile competition. Toward the end of the year, he won the Juvenile Men's competition in the Eastern Great Lakes Region. In 1971, he moved up from Juvenile to Intermediate and won the Eastern

Great Lakes championship.

In 1972, when Scott was 13, judges and skating experts told Dorothy and Ernie that Scott needed to leave Bowling Green and get better coaching elsewhere if he were to reach his potential. That summer, Scott moved to Rockton, Illinois, to take lessons from former Olympic champion Pierre Brunet at the Wagon Wheel Skating Club.

Brunet's teaching greatly improved Scott's skating. He also benefited from training with one of Brunet's other students, Gordie McClelland, who won three senior U.S. titles while Scott was there. Scott made his national debut as a novice in 1973, and in 1975 he moved up to juniors and finished seventh.

Unfortunately, Coach Brunet decided to retire in mid-1975, and Scott's friend Gordie retired from amateur skating. Scott hired new coaches Mary Ludington and Dick Scovald, who later taught Paul Wylie and Nancy Kerrigan. However, within a year Mary and Dick moved to Wisconsin. It was a very unsettling time for Scott.

And things were even more unsettled back in Bowling Green. Dorothy had been diagnosed with cancer. In addition, the family realized it had run out of money for training. The 1976 season would have to be Scott's last year on the ice. He made plans to attend Bowling Green University the next fall.

Scott was very sad when he headed to the 1976 junior nationals in Colorado Springs, Colorado. He figured it would be his last competition.

There, however, Dorothy had a surprise for him. Carlo Fassi, the man who had trained Olympic champions Peggy Fleming and Dorothy Hamill, was interested in coaching him at the

After Hamilton won his first world title in 1981, he was congratulated by his coach, Don Laws.

Broadmoor Skating Club. Better yet, a wealthy couple from Chicago had offered to pay for Scott's training and expenses. They did not allow Scott to make their names public. The only other thing his "angels" asked was that Scott work hard.

After hearing his mother's surprise, Scott was ready to hit the ice. He went out and won the 1976 U.S. junior championship—the first of what was to be many national titles to come.

Scott's small size turned out to his benefit as

Hamilton took the gold at the 1984 Olympics in Sarajevo, Yugoslavia.

a skater. In figure skating as well as in gymnastics and diving, the smaller you are, the easier it is to spin. Even medium-sized athletes find it hard to do the quick rotations that these sports prize. Also, while larger athletes may be able to jump higher, a small person's jump may seem more impressive. Thus if you watched a six-foot-tall skater jump 35 inches and then watched the 5' 3" Scott Hamilton jump 33 inches, it would seem as if Hamilton had actually leaped higher, especially in comparison to his height.

Hamilton's low weight also allowed him to zip around the rink, performing leaps and fancy footwork at breakneck speed. He could throw his body around in ways that larger skaters never could. True, larger skaters tended to be more powerful, but they had no advantage when it came to stamina. Other small skaters might get tired after a long routine, but not Scott. His ability to keep focused and in control even at the end of a strenuous and pressure-packed five-minute program was a major reason for his success.

Scott moved up to seniors in 1977, where he finished ninth. He was terribly disappointed to have skated poorly in front of his mother. She was so sick, he was afraid he would never get to show her he could do better. Sadly, Scott was right. Dorothy died on May 19, 1977.

Scott was heartbroken. He decided to throw himself into training. It would help him deal with his grief, and he could dedicate any successes to Dorothy's memory.

Now his climb to the top started going faster. In 1978, he finished third at senior nationals— a huge jump from the previous year. That earned him a spot on the U.S. team that went to the worlds. Scott finished 11th, a respectable placing.

But more disruption was around the corner. He learned while training for the 1979 season that Fassi also was going to coach Scott Cramer, one of his chief rivals. He lost trust in his coach. Then Scott tore ligaments in his ankle and was out of action much of the summer. He ended up finishing fourth at the 1979 nationals, which meant he missed making the world team by one place.

Scott decided he had to find a new coach. He settled on Don Laws, who was based in Philadelphia. It was a perfect fit. Scott trusted Don, and they liked each other. Don would remain his coach for the rest of his amateur career.

And what a career it was. The short, thin skater with the sandy hair made his first big splash in the fall of 1979. That's when he won the Flaming Leaves competition in Lake Placid, New York, the site where the Olympic Games were scheduled to take place the following year. (The competition has grown quite famous since then under the name Skate America.) Among those he defeated were the U.S. and world champions.

The next year was even better. Scott placed third at the nationals and then placed fifth at both the Olympic Winter Games in Lake Placid and the world championships. The entire U.S. Olympic team honored him by picking him to carry the American flag in the opening ceremonies. For American fans, the sight of little Scott wearing a 10-gallon cowboy hat much too big for his head and carrying a flag that seemed too long for his arms was one of the best moments of the Olympics.

"The team had this meeting about who to pick—it's a terrific honor, you know," Scott said. "And someone made this emotional pitch for me, pointing out that I had overcome terrible obstacles, sickness and all, and that my mom had died at a crucial point in my career; and that I was the smallest male Olympian there. And suddenly there I was marching along and peering out from under the rim of this cowboy hat a couple sizes too big, leading the parade into the stadium.

"I was so proud."

There would be more such moments in the four years to come. In the winter of 1981, Scott won the senior men's Eastern championship and then went on to a showdown at nationals with David Santee, the favorite.

Both skaters presented very flashy, daring long programs. David went first, gave a great performance, and got fine scores from the judges. Then Scott came out and electrified the crowd with incredibly fast skating and spins, tricky footwork, and an expressive yet very athletic and masculine style. The judges gave him just high enough scores so that he beat Santee.

His victory at nationals proved to be the second in a winning streak that wouldn't end until he reached 17 straight and turned pro. Some of those triumphs came easily, but some came very hard.

None was harder than the 1984 Olympics in Sarajevo, Yugoslavia.

The first obstacle Scott had to overcome was the pressure of being the favorite. The second was an ear infection he developed just before competition began. The third was the brilliant free skating of the fast-improving Brian Orser of Canada.

Hamilton did extremely well in the opening round of compulsory school figures, building a large lead. Orser did not do well in tracing designs on the ice, but he finished first in the short program to pull into fifth place going into the finals.

Then came the long free skating program, and that's when things really got tough. When Scott jumped, he was crooked in the air—a result of

After Hamilton turned pro, he became the most popular and highest-paid male in figure skating.

balance problems caused by the ear infection. The judges gave him good scores for his artistic merit but had to deduct points for the seeming defects in his technique. Orser skated a better long program, but the huge lead Scott had built up in compulsories was too much for him to overcome. Hamilton got the Olympic gold medal.

"It wasn't my best, but I did it," he said. "That's the way the game is scored."

Scott went on to win his fourth world title a couple of weeks later and retired from amateur skating. Soon after he turned professional and skated for two years with the Ice Capades.

Scott had never liked all the sequins and razzle-dazzle of ice skating costumes. During his long reign as world champion he wore skating suits without sequins or gold. They were designed specially to look more like those of speed skaters. He has been able to emphasize that look as a pro.

Since 1986, fans have been able to watch Scott in his own ice show, Scott Hamilton's America Tour, and in Discover Stars on Ice. In 1997, his career was interrupted by a struggle with cancer. His many fans were overjoyed when he returned to the ice in the fall, and they look forward to watching him whirl, spin, flip, and jump for years to come.

THE BATTLE OF THE BRIANS

After Scott Hamilton retired in 1984, Brian Orser was the likely heir apparent as world champion. He already was a four-time Canadian champion and had been steadily climbing the international standings for some time. Judges were well aware of this short, slender skater with fair skin and thick curly hair.

Brian, who was born on December 18, 1961, in Belleville, Ontario, made his first big splash in 1982, when he finished fourth to Scott at the world championships. He was 20 years old. The next year, 1983, he moved up another step and took the bronze medal.

Then, in the 1984 Olympics at Sarajevo, Yugoslavia, he did something no one else had been able to do in some time. He beat Scott in the free skating portions of the competition. Scott still won the gold because he was so much better at compulsories, but Brian had served notice

Brian Boitano's style was always a real crowd-pleaser.

he wanted the throne as soon as Scott left it. He also took the silver medal behind Scott at the 1984 world championships.

Orser was a great candidate. He was an expressive skater, one able to tell a story on ice. He also was an excellent athlete. His jumps were high and the landings were accurate. He only had two weaknesses: despite a lot of hard work, his ability at compulsory figures was only adequate, and he had a tendency to let his nerves get the best of him during competitions.

But as you read in history books, heirs apparent aren't always the men and women who go on to become the kings and queens. There have been many wars fought over thrones, and that was what was about to happen in international men's figure skating, an Ice War.

Orser had two primary challengers for the title of best male skater. One was an American, Brian Boitano of Sunnyvale, California, near San Francisco. The other was Alexandr Fadeev, who came from the former Communist nation called the Union of Soviet Socialist Republics (USSR), or Soviet Union for short. He was born in the city of Tashkent in the part of the USSR now known as Uzbekistan.

Boitano also was fair and had curly dark hair, though he was about a head taller than Orser. He had made his world debut with a seventh-place finish in 1983. Then in 1984, he finished fifth in the Olympics and sixth at the worlds. Both Boitano and Fadeev were 22, two years younger than Orser.

Brian Boitano was known as a jumping machine. With his powerful, long arms and long legs, he could jump higher than anyone. And he could do a triple version of every possible jump

Experts predicted Brian Orser would become a dominating skater, but he stumbled in several of his most important competitions.

consistently. His other big strength was his consistency. He never fell. The only knock about him was that he showed no personality when he skated.

The blond-haired Fadeev looked more like a wrestler than a skater. He was very small with very short, powerful legs. But the odd proportions of his body disappeared when he got on the ice, for he was both artistic and athletic. Like all Soviet skaters, he had studied dance with the famous Bolshoi ballet. His body line was perfect. So were his figures. The Soviet government lavishly supported the needs of its top athletes. As long as they performed well, their needs would continue to be met. But once they started to disappoint, that support could be yanked away.

Brian Orser was the favorite when the 1985 world championships began in Tokyo. However, his compulsory figures were so bad that he virtually lost all chance of winning that first day. He was brilliant free skating in the short and long programs, but it was not enough to overcome the big lead Fadeev had taken in figures. Brian Orser had to settle for the silver medal, and Brian Boitano, who still had trouble expressing himself on ice, won the bronze.

Orser went home and worked very hard on his compulsory figures. He also started meeting with sports psychologist Peter Jensen to try to learn how to control his butterflies and focus on his skating in competitions.

Of course, Fadeev and Boitano were working hard, too. But Orser went to the 1986 world championships thinking he could win.

He did much better than usual in figures, finishing third behind Fadeev. Fadeev kept his lead in the short program and Orser remained in third, while Brian Boitano moved up to fourth—in challenging position at least for the silver and perhaps even the gold if other skaters didn't do their best.

Alexandr's solid lead gave him the opportunity to skate for the title. Brian Orser could only win the gold medal if his Soviet competitor faltered in the long program. But that's exactly what happened: Fadeev fell twice and messed up the landings of three other jumps.

Sadly for Orser, he too fell doing a triple axel early in the program. He tried to do another later in the routine, but he came out of it too early.

Brian Boitano ended up being the surprise winner of the 1986 world championship. He landed five impressive triple jumps. His performance still wasn't very dramatic, but he skated without mistakes. That was enough to make him champion. Brian Orser finished second, and Fadeev finished third.

After collecting his third straight world silver medal, Brian Orser promised not to retire from amateur skating until he had a gold medal too. "I'll win it. It's there," he said. "I'm not quitting until I do."

Orser made good on his promise in the 1987 world championships at Riverfront Coliseum in Cincinnati, Ohio.

"I walked into the arena as if I owned the place," Orser said.

At the start of the long program, Fadeev again was first, Boitano was second, and Orser was in third. Once again, Fadeev could not keep his lead, falling on a triple axel.

Brian Boitano, still trying to inject more personality into his skating, became the first person ever to complete a quadruple jump in competition. But it was not quite the jump he wanted or needed; he bobbled the landing.

Orser finally gave the performance of his lifetime. He made no mistakes and his artistry wowed the crowd. He got seven of nine first-place votes from the judges.

Three different world champions in three years. Couldn't anyone take over men's skating and dominate it the way Dick Button, the Jenkins brothers, and Scott Hamilton had?

The answer was a year away. Nineteen eighty-eight was an Olympic year, and if one of those three skaters could win both the Olympics and the worlds, he would be remembered as the best.

The Winter Games were to be held in Calgary, in the western province of Alberta, Canada. Many members of the American and Canadian news media thought Orser would have a sort of "home-field advantage," skating in front of his fellow Canadians and perhaps with judges going easy on the hometown favorite.

The American press, though, was not about to write off its own main hope for a gold medal in figure skating. They tended to overlook Alexandr Fadeev as a legitimate contender and started to hype what became known as "The Battle of the Brians."

And that's exactly what it was. By the night of the long program, all the other competitors were just skating for the bronze medal and position. Barring some unforeseen disaster, the Brians were the only ones fighting for gold. Brian Boitano had a very slim lead going into free skating, but Brian Orser was close enough to take the gold by winning the long program.

"The Battle of the Brians" featured two skaters who had more than things in common with each other than just a first name. As fate would have it, each skater had chosen to skate impersonating a 19th-century soldier. Brian Boitano's character was a lieutenant in Napoleon's army skating to music from the movie *Napoleon*. Brian Orser was a soldier from the same era skating to music called "The Bolt."

Brian Boitano wore a royal blue uniform trimmed with gold braid. Brian Orser wore a red uniform trimmed with gold.

Boitaino skated before Orser, and his performance left the crowd and judges speechless. As usual, his jumps were technically perfect. So, too, were his spins and spirals and spread eagles and footwork. But what was really amazing was the amount of artistic expression he put into the program. Brian had been working very hard on his artistry with choreographer Sandra Bezic, and it showed. You could almost feel the adrenaline charging through Brian as he acted out a battle and sword flight.

Next came Orser, and he left everyone speechless too. He showed off his charismatic style, matching Boitano leap for leap. But Brian Orser

Boitano continues to skate as a professional. Here he shows off his style with Olympic champion Katarina Witt.

wasn't quite perfect. Judges noted that he bobbled slightly—very slightly—landing a jump called a triple flip. Then, near the end of his program, he turned a planned triple axel into a double. That indicated to the judges that he was getting a little tired.

The final scoring was as close as it has ever been in Olympic history. Brian Boitano took the gold medal, five judges to four. Fadeev, meanwhile, faltered badly. A new and younger Soviet named Viktor Petrenko took the bronze medal.

A few weeks later, Boitano also beat Orser at the 1988 world championships. The long Ice War was over. Brian Boitano was king.

Brian Orser turned professional almost immediately. Boitaino waited a while, but eventually he turned pro too. Both have been skating in television specials and ice shows ever since. They also participate in the many professional contests that have sprung up in the last few years.

Like John Curry, Boitano left a mark on the ice when he and Olympic champion Katarina Witt got together for a tour. What they did wasn't as risky as pairs but was more athletic than ice dancing. They called it shadow skating.

The International Skating Union allowed some professionals to regain amateur status and try for the 1994 Olympics. Brian Boitano made the American team and went to the Winter Games in Lillehammer, Norway. But he had a major error in his short program and was eliminated from medal contention. Now he's back thrilling crowds as one of the world's top pros.

THE NEW GENERATION

No sooner had Brian Boitano taken over the throne of men's amateur figure skating than he gave it up. Instead of trying to win a third world title in 1989, he turned professional. By that time, Brian Orser already had done the same.

Now who would take over as king of the sport?

Would it be Alexandr Fadeev, the onetime world champion who had gotten pushed aside by the battling Brians? Fadeev had decided to stay an amateur, and no one was a better technician, especially at compulsory figures. All he had to do was get more consistent when landing his jumps.

Or perhaps it would be Fadeev's younger Soviet teammate, Viktor Petrenko. He had skated well enough to win the bronze medals behind the two Brians at both the Olympics and the world championships. He already had a beauti-

Kurt Browning became the next dominating amateur when he won four world championships.

ful and polished skating line, and he could be expected to improve as he got older. But he was also very thin and would need to increase his strength and endurance if he were to become a dominating skater.

Americans were rooting for Christopher Bowman, who had finished a solid seventh in his Olympic debut in 1988. He had all the necessary skills. The dark-haired, handsome skater was very stylish and expressive. And he had an amazing ability to communicate with his audiences—even the judges. Bowman's problem, though, was a lack of self-discipline. He was the class clown, never taking his coach or his training seriously. His nickname in the skating world was "Bowman the Showman." In order for him to rise to the top, he would need to master another jump or two.

As it turned out, it would be none of them, though Petrenko and Bowman each would have brief moments of glory.

Instead it was another Canadian named Kurt Browning who rose to the top of skating. He gave his countrymen the kind of world domination Brian Orser had tried but failed to do. By the time Kurt turned professional in late 1994, he had won four world championships and four Canadian titles. He also enjoyed the same kind of global popularity as the two Brians and Scott Hamilton.

The son of a retired hunting guide from tiny Caroline, Alberta, in western Canada, Kurt had an air of the Wild West about him. He was brash and bold with jumps that were described in the media as "raw, confident and powerful." No wonder—he had divided his ice time between figure skating and hockey (Canada's number-one team sport) until he was 15. But despite his lack of polish, he had a wonderful presence. He related to crowds with the same good humor and breezy confidence of Scott Bowman.

But his reign at the top was not without setbacks. Poor timing and bad luck conspired to stop Kurt from winning the only other title that mattered. Though he went to three Winter Olympic Games, he never was able to bring home a single medal.

Of course, he expressed no disappointment when he failed to medal at his first Olympics, the 1988 Winter Games dominated by the Battling Brians. As he was only 21 years old, Kurt was mostly just happy to be invited to the big show. Still, he attracted attention for his athleticism and bravery—he was the only Olympic competitor to try a quadruple jump. Both Brians had been practicing quadruples but decided the jump was too risky with the gold medal on the line. Kurt had nothing to lose, so he went for it. He failed to land the quad cleanly, but he skated well enough to finish eighth anyway. And a few weeks later, he did land the first quadruple jump in competition history. He did it at the 1988 world championships in Budapest, Hungary, as he finished sixth, again behind the two Brians.

Browning knew he had much room to improve. And, by practicing from five to six-and-a-half hours a day, that's exactly what the tall (5' 10") athlete did. At the 1989 world championships, he finished fifth to Fadeev in the compulsory figures and then won the short program. That put him within easy striking distance of the gold. Fadeev again could not keep his lead, falling twice on the ice and falling to fourth in the overall standings. Browning made two mistakes on jumps in his long program, but they were easily forgivable considering how many leaps he attempted. He did a staggering total of seven triples and one quadruple. Bowman won the silver medal.

Browning was just the fourth Canadian to win the world crown in 78 years, and he gave Orser some credit. "He was an inspiration," Brown said.

The following year, the world championships were in Canada—in Halifax, Nova Scotia. That put a lot of pressure on Kurt. No Canadian man ever had won back-to-back world championships, and he had a lot of competition from Viktor Petrenko, who was skating very well. The huge home crowd went crazy when Kurt was judged the winner after a thrilling long program finale.

"It's definitely better the second time around," Kurt said. "I really worked for this one."

Kurt kept working, too. In the process, he scored more firsts. In the 1990 Nationals Cup, he pulled off daring back-to-back triple jumps on the same foot. Then, in the 1991 world championships in Munich, Germany, he became the first competitor to land three triple-triple combination jumps in one program.

He promised he had not reached his peak. "I'm never satisfied," he told the Canadian magazine *Macleans*. "Artistically, I'm still growing."

And he was. His style is much less classical than that of the two Brians, but just as pleasing and dramatic. Eventually he became quite good at telling a story on ice. Going into the 1992 Olympics, he was in his prime.

Athletically, however, Kurt's body was beginning to feel the toll of all those triple and quadruple jumps. In 1991, he developed a disc prob-

Elvis Stojko won the 1994 world championship and brought a new style to figure skating.

lem in his back while training and had to take three months off from competition. For eight weeks, he couldn't train at all. He even had to miss defending his three Canadian championships at the nationals.

Kurt kept up a good act when he got to the Winter Games in Albertville, France, but there were whispers that he wouldn't be able to skate well. Almost all athletes compete with some sort of pain, but there is no way to make up for the toll it takes on performance. Nor can an athlete make up for a lack of preparation.

You could tell from the start of the short program that Kurt was not ready to compete. He fell, he missed jumps, he skidded, and he looked almost scared as he skated. He looked just as bad in the long program two days later and finished sixth. Viktor Petrenko was the somewhat controversial winner, and American Paul Wylie had to settle for the silver medal.

Kurt was very embarrassed. "If I'd had two more weeks, I would have been in this thing," Kurt said.

He made good on that boast a few weeks later when he went to the 1992 world championships in Oakland, California. Though his back still was painful, he was much better prepared and finished second, again behind the young Petrenko.

Kurt originally had planned to retire and turn professional after the 1992 worlds, but his poor performance in Albertville made him change his mind. Under a new Olympic schedule, the next Winter Games would be in 1994—less than two years away. Even though he would be 27 by that time, Kurt decided to try once more for an Olympic medal.

Petrenko decided to turn professional after his one year at the top, but Kurt worried about the other, younger men coming up behind him. One of his top challengers lived right in Canada. Elvis Stojko, an amazing jumper who liked to use very unusual and modern choreography, was starting to look like a world beater. And you also had to watch out for rising stars like American Scott Davis, France's Philippe Candeloro, and the usual group of tough skaters from the countries that used to be the republics of the Soviet Union.

But Kurt was really motivated to win the 1993 world title. He felt it would be a way to redeem himself after the disappointing skating he did at the Olympics. He went to the championships in Prague, Czechoslovakia determined to win the gold.

And so he did, with two of the kind of programs that pull people out of their seats for a standing ovation. His short program was skated to drum music, and it was fast and exciting. Best of all, he made no mistakes and took the lead.

His long program was very different but just as good. It was set to the music theme from the movie *Casablanca,* which starred Humphrey Bogart as the lovelorn owner of a Moroccan bar during World War II. Kurt played the role as if he were Bogart's long-lost twin—right down to the way that Bogart would hold and smoke a cigarette.

Kurt became the early favorite for the 1994 Olympics in Norway, but he was no shoo-in. That year, the International Skating Union decided to allow pros to ask for reinstatement as amateurs. The 1988 Olympic champion Brian Boitano and 1992 champion Viktor Petrenko were among those who were granted amateur status.

Now Kurt would have to beat not only all the young guys coming up, but the man who beat him in 1992 and one of his role models from 1988. Because of the mix of former pros and young amateurs, the Olympics in Lillehammer, Norway, promised to be one of the most exciting competitions of all time.

And it was. But the outcome of the men's competition was very shocking. In some ways, the

Philippe Candeloro is one of several young stars looking to become the next great skater.

outcome was decided the very first night, during the short program.

That night, all the established stars made big mistakes—so big they put themselves pretty much out of reach for any medals. Kurt had a very bad night. He fell on a triple jump and turned a required double axel into a single. He finished the night in 12th place.

Boitano and Petrenko looked rusty after not having competed for so long. They stood eighth and ninth going into the free skating, or long program, final. It appeared that the newest, youngest challengers to the throne would win the medals. First was Aleksei Urmanov, a 20-year-old Russian. Elvis Stojko stood second, and Phillippe Candeloro of France was third.

The old guys didn't go down easily, though. Browning landed six clean triples in his Bogart program. Petrenko did seven. Boitano did five. Their performances pulled them up in the standings, but not quite enough. Petrenko finished fourth overall; Kurt was fifth, and Brian Boitano was sixth.

The gold medal went to Aleksei; Elvis took the silver; and Phillippe won the bronze.

Afterward, Kurt finally turned professional, and Brian and Viktor also returned to the pro ranks. Kurt has been starring with Scott Hamilton and Kristi Yamaguchi in the touring show Stars on Ice since 1995.

In amateur skating, though, another Ice War has been going on. And there seem to be many pretenders to the throne.

Elvis Stojko won the 1994 and 1995 world titles, but he lost all chance of winning in 1996 when he fell during his short program. The world title went to American Todd Eldredge. Ilia Kulik, 18, of Russia was second. The bronze went to Rudy Galindo, a veteran American skater who had won top medals both as a singles skater and in pairs. For many years he had partnered Kristi Yamaguchi, who herself became a champion singles skater. Rudy turned pro a few months later.

As the 20th century draws to a close, Elvis Stojko and Todd Eldredge are among the favorites in world amateur competition—but there are sure to be some young, lesser-known talents just waiting for their moment of glory.

CHRONOLOGY

1908 Ulrich Salchow of Sweden wins the first Olympic figure-skating competition.

1920 Gillis Grafstrom of Sweden wins the first of three consecutive Olympic gold medals.

1932 Karl Schaefer of Austria wins the first of two consecutive Olympic gold medals.

1948 Dick Button becomes the first American to win gold at the Olympics.

1952 Dick Button successfully defends his Olympic title.

1956 Hayes Alan Jenkins of the U.S. wins the Olympic gold.

1960 David Jenkins, Hayes's younger brother, takes the Olympic title.

1976 John Curry of Great Britain wins the Olympic gold.

1984 Scott Hamilton reclaims the Olympic title for the United States.

1988 Brian Boitano wins the gold in one of the tightest Olympic finishes.

1992 Viktor Petrenko wins the gold, and fellow Russian Alexei Urmanov defends the title at the Olympics two years later.

FURTHER READING

Brennan, Christine. *Inside Edge*. New York: Random House, 1993.

Button, Dick. *Dick Button on Skates*. Engleside Cliffs, NJ: Prentice Hall, 1955.

Fassi, Carlo, with Gregory Smith. *Figure Skating with Carlo Fassi*. New York: Scribner, 1980.

Gutman, Dan. *Ice Skating: From Axels to Zambonis*. New York: Viking Press, 1995.

Jonland, Einar, with Jim Fitzgerald. *Inside Ice Skating*. Chicago: Contemporary Books, 1978.

ABOUT THE AUTHOR

Pohla Smith has been a journalist for 25 years. She was a writer and columnist for United Press International from 1973-1991, specializing in figure skating, gymnastics, and horse racing over her last decade with the wire service. Recently, Ms. Smith has been teaching at the University of Pittsburgh and acting as writing coach/assistant metro editor for *The North Hills News Record*, a Gannett newspaper. Ms. Smith's work frequently is seen in *Sports Illustrated for Kids* and *USA Today*. She is the author of *Superstars of Women's Gymnastics* and *Head-to-Head Basketball: Shaquille O'Neal and Hakeem Olajuwon*.

INDEX

Bezic, Sandra, 49
Boitano, Brian, 44-51, 53, 59, 60
Bowman, Christopher, 54, 55
Brennan, Christine, 26
Browning, Kurt, 53, 54-59
Brunet, Pierre, 34
Button, Dick, 7-11, 13, 14-15, 18-19
Candeloro, Philippe, 58, 60
Cramer, Scott, 37
Curry, John, 23-29, 51
Davis, Scott, 58
Eldredge, Todd, 61
Fadeev, Alexandr, 44-47, 48, 50, 53, 55
Fassi, Carlo, 34, 37
Fleming, Dorothy, 11, 35
Galindo, Rudy, 61
Grafstrom, Gillis, 24
Grogan, Jimmy, 15
Hamill, Dorothy, 8, 35
Hamilton, Dorothy, 31-33, 34-35, 37
Hamilton, Ernie, 31-33, 34
Hamilton, Scott, 31-41, 43-44, 60

Hamilton, Susan, 32, 33
Heiss, Carol, 21
Jenkins, David, 13-21
Jenkins, Hayes Alan, 13-21
Jenkins, Nancy, 14
Jensen, Peter, 46
Klepner, Andrew, 32-33
Kulik, Ilia, 61
Laws, Don, 35, 38
Lussi, Gus, 7-8, 14
Mosler, Ed, 25, 27
Orser, Brian, 39-40, 43-51, 53, 56
Petrenko, Viktor, 48, 50, 53-54, 56, 58, 59, 60
Santee, David, 39
Shwachmann, Harry, 33
Starbuck, JoJo, 28
Stojko, Elvis, 57, 58, 60, 61
Tharp, Twyla, 27
Urmanov, Aleksei, 60
Witt, Katarina, 50, 51
Wylie, Paul, 26, 58
Yamaguchi, Kristi, 60

PICTURE CREDITS:
All photos in this book are from AP/Wide World Photos.